Corn Snakes as Pets

Caring For Your Corn Snake

Corn Snake facts, care, breeding, nutritional information, tips, and more!

By Lolly Brown

Foreword

Having unusual pets such as snakes can become challenging. For people who want to experience keeping snakes as pets, the Corn Snake from North America is a popular option. In fact, it is one of the best snakes to keep as a pet. They are small to medium-sized snakes, usually around three to five feet – large enough to handle, but not as intimidating as other snake species can be.

Corn snakes are also docile compared to other species and if the amateur snake keeper is not careful enough and encounters an accident, they can rest easy as Corn Snakes are not venomous. Corn Snakes are indeed a great start for individuals interested and want to learn more about snakes. As you read this book, you will learn about what it takes to keep a Corn Snake as a house pet, and how to keep them happy.

Embark on a wonderful journey of sharing your life with a Corn Snake. Learn to maximize the great privilege of living with one and be able to share this unique and unforgettable experience just like many pet snake owners that came before you!

Table of Contents

Introduction

When people think of pets, the first ones that come to mind are the classic choices – cats, dogs, birds, hamsters, and other usual domesticated animals. Well, we can safely assume that you are obviously interested in snakes or have already had previous experience in handling one before that's why you're reading this book – and that's awesome! Keep reading!

Pantherophis guttatus, more commonly known as the Corn Snake, gets its name from the corn-like pattern on its skin. Its belly in particular looks similar to Indian corn. In the wild, their colors are combinations of yellow, orange, brown, and black.

Corn snakes are native to the southeastern portion of the United States and are relatively small and harmless as they are non-venomous, making it the perfect pet snake for the beginner snake keeper.

This species is a member of the Colubridea family; the most common family of snakes, which Encyclopedia Britannica defines as "characterized by the complete absence of hind limbs, the absence or considerable reduction of the left lung, and the lack of teeth on the premaxilla and usually having a loose facial structure, relatively few head scales, and ventral scales as wide as the body." This family of snakes also includes Corn Snakes, milk snakes, and rat snakes. However, one must still take caution in caring for a corn snake. While they are non-venomous, the corn snake subdues its prey by constriction. And of course, it doesn't hurt to be extra-careful of bites, too.

This book will guide you on what a corn snake needs and exercising caution in approaching your pet or soon-to-be pet. You will learn their behaviors, what to watch out for, what to feed them, and what you need to be a responsible keeper. It will also provide information you need to know to decide whether or not you want to take care of this fascinating pet. Turn the page to start learning more about the attractive and friendly corn snake! The serpent world awaits!

Glossary of Snake Terms

1.2.3. (Numbers with full stops) – The numbers are used to denote the number of a species, arranged according to sex, thus: male.female.unknown sex. In this case, one male, two females, and three of unknown sex.

Acclimation – Adjusting to a new environment or new conditions over a period of time.

Active range – The area of activity which can include hunting, seeking refuge, and finding a mate.

Ambient temperature – The overall temperature of the environment.

Amelanistic – Amel for short; without melanin, or without any black or brown coloration.

Anal Plate – A modified ventral scale that covers and protects the vent; sometimes a single plate, sometimes a divided plate.

Anerythristic – Anery for short; without any red coloration.

Aquatic – Lives in water.

Arboreal – Lives in trees.

Betadine – An antiseptic that can be used to clean wounds in reptiles.

Bilateral – Where stripes, spots or markings are present on both sides of an animal.

Biotic – The living components of an environment.

Brille – A transparent scale above the eyes of snakes that allows them to see but also serves to protect the eyes at the same time. Also called Spectacle, and Ocular Scale.

Brumation – The equivalent of mammalian hibernation among reptiles.

Cannibalistic – Where an animal feeds on others of its own kind.

Caudocephalic Waves – The ripple-like contractions that move from the rear to the front of a snake's body.

CB – Captive Bred, or bred in captivity.

CH – Captive Hatched.

Cloaca – also Vent; a half-moon shaped opening for digestive waste disposal and sexual organs.

Cloacal Gaping – Indication of sexual receptivity of the female.

Cloacal Gland – A gland at the base of the tail which emits foul smelling liquid as a defense mechanism; also called Anal Gland.

Clutch – A batch of eggs.

Constriction – The act of wrapping or coiling around a prey to subdue and kill it prior to eating.

Crepuscular – Active at twilight, usually from dusk to dawn.

Crypsis – Camouflage or concealing.

Diurnal – Active by day

Drop – To lay eggs or to bear live young.

Ectothermic – Cold-blooded. An animal that cannot regulate its own body temperature, but sources body heat from the surroundings.

Endemic – Indigenous to a specific region or area.

Estivation – Also Aestivation; a period of dormancy that usually occurs during the hot or dry seasons in order to escape the heat or to remain hydrated.

Faunarium (Faun) – A plastic enclosure with an air holed lid, usually used for small animals such as hatchling snakes, lizards, and insects.

FK – Fresh Killed; a term usually used when feeding a rodent that is recently killed, and therefore still warm, to a pet snake.

Flexarium – A reptile enclosure that is mostly made from mesh screening, for species that require plenty of ventilation.

Fossorial – A burrowing species.

Fuzzy – For rodent prey, one that has just reached the stage of development where fur is starting to grow.

F/T – Frozen/thawed; used to refer to food items that are frozen but thawed before feeding to your pet.

Gestation – The period of development of an embryo within a female.

Gravid – The equivalent of pregnant in reptiles.

Glottis – A tube-like structure that projects from the lower jaw of a snake to facilitate ingestion of large food items.

Gut-loading – Feeding insects within 24 hours to a prey before they are fed to your pet, so that they pass on the nutritional benefits.

Hatchling – A newly hatched, or baby, reptile.

Hemipenes – Dual sex organs; common among male snakes.

Hemipenis – A single protrusion of a paired sexual organ; one half is used during copulation.

Herps/Herpetiles – A collective name for reptile and amphibian species.

Herpetoculturist – A person who keeps and breeds reptiles in captivity.

Herpetologist – A person who studies ectothermic animals, sometimes also used for those who keeps reptiles.

Herpetology – The study of reptiles and amphibians.

Hide Box – A furnishing within a reptile cage that gives the animal a secure place to hide.

Hots – Venomous.

Husbandry – The daily care of a pet reptile.

Hygrometer – Used to measure humidity.

Impaction – A blockage in the digestive tract due to the swallowing of an object that cannot be digested or broken down.

Incubate – Maintaining eggs in conditions favorable for development and hatching.

Interstitial – The skin between scales.

Intromission – Also mating; when the male's hemipenis is inserted into the cloaca of the female.

Juvenile – Not yet adult; not of breedable age.

LTC – Long Term Captive; or one that has been in captivity for more than six months.

MBD – Metabolic Bone Disease; occurs when reptiles lack sufficient calcium in their diet.

Morph – Color pattern

Musking – Secretion of a foul smelling liquid from its vent as a defense mechanism.

Oviparous – Egg-bearing.

Ovoviviparous – Eggs are retained inside the female's body until they hatch.

Pinkie – Newborn rodent.

Pip – The act of a hatchling snake to cut its way out of the egg using a special egg tooth.

PK – Pre-killed; a term used when live rodents are not fed to a snake.

Popping – The process by which the sex is determined among hatchlings.

Probing – The process by which the sex is determined among adults.

Regurgitation – Also Regurge; occurs when a snake regurgitates or brings out a half-digested meal.

R.I. – Respiratory Infection; common condition among reptiles kept in poor conditions.

Serpentine Locomotion – The manner in which snakes move.

Sloughing – Shedding.

Sub-adult – Juvenile.

Substrate – The material lining the bottom of a reptile enclosure.

Stat – Short for Thermostat

Tag – Slang for a bite or being bitten

Terrarium – A reptile enclosure.

Thermo-regulation – The process by which cold-blooded animals regulate their body temperature by moving from hot to cold surroundings.

Vent – Cloaca

Vivarium – Glass-fronted enclosure

Viviparous – Gives birth to live young.

WC – Wild Caught.

Weaner – A sub-adult rodent.

WF – Wild Farmed; refers to the collection of a pregnant female whose eggs or young were hatched or born in captivity.

Yearling – A year old.

Zoonosis – A disease that can be passed from animal to man.

Chapter One: Corn Snake in Focus

Corn Snakes can be your best friend. People love them for their beauty and docile temperament. Some people even sleep and eat with them which just show that Corn Snakes are indeed a great companion. They can definitely meet your basic psychological needs in pretty much the way humans do. They can make you feel socially content, with the result of feeling better about life in general. Isn't that amazing?

The Corn Snakes are very interesting in both personality and aesthetics and can really be a great pet but it is recommended that you research first before getting one because owning one is not something that you can just assume or overlooked.

The next section will give you an overview of the Corn Snakes and some of its interesting facts. It will also guide you on the decision of owning one as having this type of pet is something really cool!

Facts about Corn Snakes

Pantherophis guttatus or the Corn Snake is recognized by its corn kernel-like scales. They come in combinations of yellow, orange, brown, and black, and its belly looks similar to Indian corn. They are a rodent-eating species native to the Southeastern and Central United States.

The Corn Snake did not just earn its name from its appearance. Southern farmers used to store harvested corn in a crib – a wood frame or log building. Rats and mice came there to eat the corn, and the corn snakes came to eat the rats and mice that gathered there. The snakes were able to stay and hide on the logs while enjoying the rodents that came to eat the corn.

With proper care, a corn snake may live for 20 years even in captivity. They are also start reproducing around 10 to 12 years, sometimes even longer. They hatch at 8 to 12 inches long and adults range from 2.5 to 5 feet long. In the wild, they eat lizards, rodents and birds, while in captivity they can live on a diet of mice and small rats.

The Corn Snake is also referred to as the Red Rat Snake or Jungle Corn Snake, and it is a constrictor-type. Since they are not venomous, the corn snake wraps its body around its prey or enemy before biting. While pure corn snakes are not venomous, hybrids created in captivity or in the wild may be venomous and their venom may even be toxic enough to cause death.

Potential and starting keepers alike are fascinated by their colors and patterns. At the same time, corn snakes are relatively easy to care for as they are a hardy species – they don't get sick easily – and can tolerate handling by its keepers. They are also very docile which makes them a good snake for the amateur snake keeper. However, because they can live long, you may want to consider the future if you want to take care of a corn snake. Keeping a corn snake is a long-term commitment.

Getting Ready to Commit

While corn snakes make great snakes to keep as pets, one must still make sure they are ready to commit to taking care of one. Like usual house pets, snakes are not accessories

– they are living, breathing animals. Each one has its own personality, and it takes time to get to know your pet snake. Once you have chosen to keep it, it will take some time for it to get used to you.

That is why it's very important to research first all the information about Corn Snakes before deciding to own one. It's something that you have to do. The first thing that you need to consider about snakes is they are not dogs or cats or fish or birds or guinea pig or any other animal. They are something different. They are snakes. A snake is an animal that has to be respected, for it to respect you back. Think of it as some sort of (deadly) weapon in Martial Arts. If you don't respect your weapon, it may harm you. "It's a double-edged sword," either it could defend you or kill you. It is the same with snakes or any other animals as well. You can't just train it to behave the way that you want it to behave. You have to respect its behavior. If it doesn't like to be handled then don't handle it. If it bites you, you can't punish it.

It's also very important to figure out the reason why you want it. If you just want a snake because it looks awesome and it will project you as someone who is fearless or it's like an awesome fashion statement, don't do it. Just go buy necklace or a pair of shoes or something. A snake is a living animal. It's not some just an accessory. You have to care for it, and love it and nurture it and look after it and everything else. They are a living creature and you can't just buy one just because you have an epic vision of you lying in your bed being in all sexy with your pet snake.

Next thing you should need to figure out is the age you want to buy. Baby snakes are referred to as hatchlings. The younger that you start handling a snake generally the better temperament they will have for the rest of their lives. You should also consider their feeding habit, where to buy a reputable one, and also their shedding routines and schedule. There's obviously a lot more about owning a Corn Snakes.

Snakes don't easily get used to being transferred so take this into consideration when thinking of buying one – are you the type to move around, or are you living in a permanent home? Do you have enough space for an aquarium large enough to accommodate it? Can your budget handle the addition to your household? Consider the possible changes in your lifestyle and carefully assess the risks, pros, and cons. These will be discussed in this book so keep reading to see if the Corn Snake is the right pet for you!

Quick Facts

Scientific Name: *Pantherophis guttatus*

Size as they hatch from their eggs: 8 to 12 inches.

Maximum adult size: 6 feet in length

Average size: 2 to 6 feet

Birth Date: Unknown

Wild Diet: Lizards, rodents, and birds.

Museum Diet: Mice and small rats.

Life Span in the Wild: 10 to 20 years

Life Span in Captivity: 20 to 25 years

Habitat: Pine forests, rocky outcrops, grasslands, hills and around farms and grain stores

Distribution and Range: North, Southeastern, and Central America.

Chapter Two: Corn Snake Requirements

Are you now thinking of getting a Corn Snake as a pet? Fantastic! Still quite weird, but unique! After knowing what they are, their characteristics, and how to deal with them, it's time to give you practical tips on what you need to know before buying one.

In this chapter, you will get a whole lot of information on its pros and cons, its average associated costs as well as the legal licensing you need so that you will be well on your way to becoming a legitimate Corn Snake pet owner – should you decide to be one! Let's do this!

First of all, you should ask yourself exactly why you want to keep a Corn Snake as a pet. Corn Snake has an average lifespan of 20 - 25 years! It's like raising a child or getting married. But if you are only considering getting a Corn Snake as a status symbol, then you should rethink your choices. As much as Corn Snake would make a wonderful addition to your household with their natural elegance and exquisiteness, their care would also demand much of your commitment. The responsibilities you would have to carry include feeding them, cleaning after them, seeing to their maintenance, and understanding their behavior.

Corn Snake although most of the time a calm and docile pet, it still has an aggressiveness that you don't want to see (after all they are still snakes), and their defense mechanism may involve a lot of eating, even their own kind, so please feed them properly. However Corn Snakes also responds very well to human touch especially if it is constant, so you would have to make sure that you do not neglect them. They are not picky eaters but it can definitely bite or harm you, so please watch out. You will also have to check them constantly for ticks and mites and their overall health.

Simply put, Corn Snakes requires a fair amount of guarantee that you will be there to take care of them and make sure they are okay. You cannot take care of a Corn Snake halfway, and you have to be all in – starting with recognizing within yourself if you have what it takes to take care of this lovely and royal creature.

License Requirements

Unlike venomous snakes, you do not need a license to keep a corn snake. In fact, the corn snake is one of the most docile snake species!

As a reminder there is no federal law governing private possession or ownership of exotic animals in the United States. You need to pay attention not on a national level but on a local level, with your local and state laws and ordinances, to see what is permitted and what is not.

The regulations vary from one city/state to another, as some outright ban or prohibit exotic or dangerous animals, while others simply call for permits that set down requirements such as micro-chipping, an established relationship with a veterinarian, and even insurance. Some may also ask you to present proof that you are acquiring the animal from a recognized breeder and that the snake was bred in captivity (as opposed to being captured from the wild), so acquiring a license from the Office of Environment and Heritage can really help.

It is also a good idea to check the rules about keeping pet snakes based on where you are - city, town, neighborhood, and even in the apartment building, if applicable. All these are reasonable precautions to take simply for the fact that should you ever be found to be keeping such a pet illegally, the discovery could result in consequences such as fines or, worse, the confiscation of your pet. You might not even be able to find a veterinarian willing to give your Corn Snake medical care if you are found to be keeping it without the correct permits. (Yeah, human can be quite cruel too, but it's protocol.)

Permits may also be necessary for importing, exporting, or traveling with an exotic or a naturally dangerous animal, especially in United Kingdom or Asia.

You also need to be constantly updated on information regarding your local state laws at least once every six months. Regulations can change, and you don't want to find yourself suddenly in violation of a law which was amended after you thought you had abided by it a year ago.

If all this seems complicated and really overwhelming, you have to remind yourself that you are bringing a potentially dangerous animal into a human community. One that can definitely eat anyone alive! As such, restrictions and limitations should be expected so that the safety of anyone involved will be ensured.

It must also be noted as a point of fact that the illegal trade in exotic animals has been an immensely profitable business for backyard breeders and illegal importers. If you care about these animals at all, you shouldn't support activities which promote their unlawful capture from the wild or the breeding and transport of these animals in inappropriate and pitiless conditions.

As mentioned earlier, like most snakes, Corn Snakes are still carnivorous and may be agitated when handled carelessly. One must know how to approach their pet and respect their corn snake's space. We have to keep in mind that our scaly friend has moods. Just like any living creature, they may turn hostile with enough provocation. It is just like having a roommate – be careful not to do anything to make them feel threatened, and remember to give them some space. Respect them, and all will be well.

In this chapter, we will discuss how to build and maintain a home for your corn snake, what to feed your snake, behaviors to watch out for, and the positive and negative things about welcoming a corn snake into your home.

How Many Corn Snakes Should You Keep?

The answer lies within you! Of course it would be great to have more so that your pet snake will have a companion in this "human or humane world."

Just like when considering other pets, the decision of whether you can keep more than one Corn Snake or not depends on your overall capacity to commit to all of them. Although, it's probably better to separate them from one another to avoid competition or showmanship, and to keep them from destroying one another or conspired against you.

Of course, you must also keep in mind that keeping more than one Corn Snake means an increase in responsibility financially, timewise, and even mentally.

Efforts of cleanup and cage maintenance will be doubled, or tripled, and can definitely take up all your time. Before committing to it, you should assess your capacity (financially, mentally and timely) to provide what your pets will require without fail. You will have to be completely ready and prepared because you're about to "raise a child"!

Taking care of one Corn Snake is already a lot, especially if this is your first time owning a snake as a pet. Be sure to make an informed and responsible decision on how many Corn Snake you can responsibly and dutifully care for and keep.

Corn Snake with Other Pets

The Corn Snake is a carnivorous natural predator, and when in the wild, they are inclined to eat other creatures, it is basic animal instinct.

As stated before, Corn Snake are docile pets if handled and trained properly. They can be a recommended snake to have if you are looking for a really friendly reptile pet or if you're already an expert in taking care of snakes. Usually Corn Snakes will not be a threat to other pets such as cats, rabbits or dogs – as long as they don't threaten him.

It is important to prepare for the cost of having a pet snake. Not only do you have to save up to buy your corn snake, you also have to consider how much keeping it for the next few years will cost you. You have prepared your housemate, now it's time to prepare yourself financially.

In this chapter, we will discuss the average prices for materials you will need to keep your corn snake happy and safe at home.

Ease and Cost of Care

Purchase Price: $30 or more

A basic corn snake would cost you around $30. Others sell hybrids or corn snakes with unique colors and shades, and these would usually cost you around $69 or more.

Glass Aquarium: around $100

Get your corn snake a bigger tank so you won't have to replace the tank when your baby corn snake grows bigger. You can get a glass aquarium enough to house an adult corn snake, and use a screen to seal the top. You should consider getting at least a 20-gallon long aquarium, and remember: one corn snake per cage!

Under Tank Heater (UTH): $25 to $30

An under tank heater controls the temperature inside the aquarium to keep your snake comfortable. It will cost you around $25 to $30, depending on the brand and price.

Heat Lamp Setup: $50 to $75

Also serving as a heater for your snake, this set-up will set you back at least $50. You will have to change light bulbs often as they may go out after some time so expect to spend a little more.

Bedding or Substrate: $21 or more

Many corn snake keepers recommend using aspen shavings as bedding for your snake tank. A bag of 24 Quarts of aspen shavings will cost you around $21. You can opt for newspapers which may be cheaper, but your corn snake will simply go under it.

Caging Materials and Furniture: $25 to $50

Other materials and furniture such as the water bowl, branches, rocks, and more will cost you around $25 to $50. These will give your snake some hiding spaces which will help it to feel more secure in its home.

Food: $10 to $12 a month

Your corn snake will eat mice weekly, so be prepared to spend for your pet's food monthly. On average, an adult snake eats 4 to 5 adult mice a month. You may prefer to shop at local pet stores – which may cost you more but are convenient. If you do, it may set you back about $12 a month. Online, buying in bulk will cost you around 70 cents per mouse plus the shipping.

Veterinary: $75 - $125

Your corn snake will not need a lot of visits to the vet – however, you still have to take it to the vet for a check-up every once in a while. Getting a corn snake checked may cost you around $75 or more.

Emergency Costs: $800 to $1200

Even if corn snakes aren't venomous, paying for the medical cost of a snake bike still isn't cheap. While corn snakes are usually docile, you still have to consider the risk of you or someone else agitating it – of course, prevention is always better but set aside the cash just in case something happens.

Overview of Expenses

Needs	Costs
Purchase Price	$30 - $100 (£24.66 - £82.19)
Glass Aquarium	$100 (£82.19)
Under Tank Heater	$25 - $30 (£20.55 - £24.66)
Heat Lamp	$50 - $75 (£41.09 - £61.64)
Substrate	$21 - $25 (£17.26 - £20.55)
Caging Materials	$25 - $50 (£20.55 - £41.09)
Food	$10 - $12 (£8.22 - £9.86)
Veterinary Care	$75 - $125 (£61.64 - £102.74)
Total	$336- $517 (£276.16 - £424.92)

*Costs may vary depending on location
**Costs may change based on the currency exchange

Pros and Cons of Keeping Corn Snakes

Each snake breed is different. While keeping a corn snake is a good experience, it may not be for everyone. One must carefully assess the positive and negative things about keeping a snake, and the particular breed of snake they want to keep.

This section outlines the pros and cons of keeping a Corn Snake.

Pros

- Docile and easy to tame, inquisitive and active.
- Rarely bite, safe around children if supervised appropriately.
- Easy and simple to take care of, only require feeding every 5-14 days depending on age.
- Grow to a manageable size (5 to 4 feet on average).
- Relatively cheap to buy and not expensive to feed.
- Unlikely to get ill with appropriate care.
- Trouble-free feeding and shedding in captivity.
- Can live for about 15 to 20 years!

Cons

- Not as receptive to humans as other animals usually kept as pets.

- Cannot be taught to respond to their names and do tricks.

- Corn Snakes, like most snakes eat rodents so they are not recommended pets for people who may not stand feeding.

- Food only available in reptile shops and online.

- Can live up to 20 years so they may be difficult to rehome.

- Many people are afraid of snakes, so be prepared for guests who may not respond positively to your pet.

Chapter Three: Purchasing Your Corn Snake

Now that you know more about the Corn Snake, you are ready to consider the costs of keeping one and convince your family, roommates, or anyone living with you not to worry about your corn snake. You also have to consider the negative response to your pet – both from guests and your housemates. Convincing them will not be easy!

In this chapter you will find valuable information about where to find a Corn Snake breeder, how to select a reputable breeder, and the questions you need to ask from your potential supplier. You will also receive tips for your home and for introducing your new pet snake to your family.

This chapter will also discuss the different things you can do to get them to be comfortable with the idea of living with a snake at home.

Convincing Your Housemates

One of the biggest hurdles to getting a pet snake is convincing your housemates, especially if you live with your parents. The idea of keeping a snake at home is difficult to sell. To one who is not used to snakes, having one at home can be terrifying, especially if you have a phobia of snakes.

So, how does one convince their housemate to let them keep a corn snake?

Learn about corn snakes – and share what you know!

In the previous chapters, we have discussed basic facts about the corn snake. It is docile, can grow up to 5 or 6 feet, and it feeds mostly on rodents. These will come in handy when you ask your housemates or parents if they will be okay with you keeping a corn snake.

If you can, get guidebooks like this one on corn

snakes and taking care of them, so your housemate will know that they do not have to be afraid. Familiarize them with snakes by going with them to the zoo or talking to them.

Present to them the idea of having a snake at home.

Of course, you shouldn't suddenly tell them that you'll be getting a pet snake. Wait until you have familiarized them enough with snakes to be comfortable enough to entertain the idea of living with one. You should also be able to answer their questions about corn snakes about the risks of taking care of one, how much it will cost, and how big it will get. Be honest so that they will be able to assess the risks and costs of living with a pet snake.

Reassure them that you can take care of your snake.

As with all pets, you must be able to take care of your corn snake. You should have enough time to spend with your snake. Reassure your housemates that you are responsible enough to keep your snake, and that they won't end up having to feed it for you or fight it off if it escapes and becomes agitated. This can only be done by showing them, not just telling them, that you are a responsible keeper.

Try to convince them – but if you can't, don't force them.

If you've tried everything you can to convince your housemates or parents but they still don't want to live with a snake, don't force them to! Even if corn snakes aren't venomous, people who aren't prepared to live with one may in some way agitate it. Even worse, it may cause a fight between you and your housemates. We get it, it's not easy to convince people to live with a snake, but there is reason for them to be scared. Despite everything, snakes are not used to people and people are almost taught to fear snakes. So don't push it – wait until you can get your own place or find housemates willing to accommodate your corn snake.

Before you get your own corn snake, you must make sure the people you live with are okay with it. Otherwise, you might end up having to relocate it – and corn snakes aren't easy to put up for adoption like dogs and cats are.

Now, if you have convinced your housemates, read on to find out how much it costs to take care of your pet corn snake.

Finding a Reputable Corn Snake Breeder

It is indeed important that your Corn Snake should come from a reputable local breeder. These breeders must be knowledgeable about the breeds they raise and they have to know about the relevant genetics. They have to take note that the primary reason for breeding a snake is for health and appearance comes in secondary only. Some breeders are very much concerned about appearance, of course, including colors and markings, but the most elegant Corn Snake is no good if it's not healthy.

It is preferred to deal with small breeders because they're more knowledgeable about the Corn Snakes, they're selling and producing. They can teach you the complete set-ups and inform you about your species' temperaments, preferred cages and other details you need to know. Breeders tend to know a lot about the species they breed, so they often can supply more information than a typical pet store clerk. You can make a list of the breeders who specialize in Corn Snakes. This is becoming easier to do with the help of the internet.

A bit of Google search magic can help you find these people. Other places to look for breeders are the Corn Snake breeder directory and the fauna classifieds websites. Also, you can look for online communities that specialize in Corn Snakes and you'll often find that those forums have a place for people to list either businesses or individual snakes for sale. Also, the website pet-snakes.com has a list of breeders in our snakes by state section.

If you are still having some problems in finding a breeder, you may want to try contacting another breeder and asking them if they can recommend anyone to you. The reptile community group is a tight knit group and it's very common for people to recommend one another even if competition exists between the parties.

Next thing to do after making a list is contacting the breeders and start talking specifics. Get a feel for what they know about their Corn Snakes. There are some places that appear to be breeder but they are not. They may work directly with importers who provide them the animals instead of producing them in their own. There is a great chance that they might not have any information about the Corn Snakes that they are selling.

Be sure not to waste their times because they have business to run just like anyone else. It is recommended to ask relevant questions about their breeding practices. This is a relevant exercise for a few reasons:

- **It will tell you who you are doing business with**

A good breeder who is passionate about the animals that they breed will want to talk to you about them. They will not hesitate to answer your questions and at the same time ask questions of their own. If a breeder doesn't bother to answer all of your questions in order to get you to spend money with them do you think they will be responsive after the sale?

- **It establishes a relationship between yourself and the breeder:**

If you're going to spend hundreds of dollars with someone who you only know online, wouldn't you like them to know as much about you in regards to the snakes you will buy from them as possible? It sure does, and almost everyone else does as well. That is why it is very important to establish a relationship with the breeder.

- **Sometimes you'll find a better deal:**

You must not be limited to Corn Snakes listed on a breeders' website. You may need to ask the breeder if they had any other Corn Snakes other than what was listed. Those three reasons alone are sure enough to convince you that opening a dialogue between you and the snake breeder is not only a good idea, but a prudent one too.

In choosing the right breeder, you must pick the one you are most comfortable with. Your decision on which breeders you will be most comfortable buying a Corn Snake from must be based on your research and communications.

You may have a list of three or four. One is going to be the primary and the others will be "just in case". At this point, you may ask for references and sometimes, it may be good to wait. Why? Because one might be selling what they have bred for the first time and has no references at that point although they are a really good and honorable person.

Ask the reference at least three to five questions about anything you want to know about their Corn Snake. You can ask whatever questions related to the purchase of the snake. The following are some guides in asking questions to the reference:

- How many Corn Snakes have you bought from [breeder name]?

- Have you ever had any issues with DOA specimens?

- After the sale how has the communication been?

- Would you buy another snake from them right now?

- Can you provide me the contact information of anyone else you know who has bought from this snake breeder in the past?

Those are just some examples you may want to ask a reference. Bottom line is the purpose of asking questions is to make your decision easier.

At some point you'll need to decide who you will be buying your Corn Snake from. Once you've made a research on the species of snake you are interested in buying; made a list of breeders who sell Corn Snake; contact the breeders in your list; choose the breeder you are most comfortable with and finally speak to the references, then you are ready to make a purchase. Once all of the leg-work is done, purchasing the snake is the easy part, simply because you are already well-informed.

Buying a snake can be daunting, but when you find a good breeder, they will walk you through every step of the process. They are willing to answer all of your questions and if they think that you are not a good fit as an owner, they won't sell it to you. Yes, they want to earn money but they also want to protect the integrity of the hobby. That's usually a great sign that the breeder really care about the pets.

Questions to Ask From a Snake Breeder

Owners who buy straight from a breeder can likely expect to pay higher than buying from a pet store, but not always. Unlike pet shops, a breeder does not have to deal with costs of paying employees and leasing a space that leads to higher markups on animals for sale. Other breeders will also choose to sell their breeds in a cheaper price than expected to undercut their competition.

You can ask questions in order to screen breeders under consideration. Some of these questions may include:

- How many years have you been in business, and what kind of experience do you have as a breeder?

- What do you specialize in? What types of species do you breed and sell?

- Do you offer any kind of a warranty or guarantee?

- Who are your customers?

- Have you received any complaints or negative feedback online or from the Better Business Bureau?

- Can you provide the names and numbers of at least three recent private individuals you have sold to, who I can contact to gauge their satisfaction in buying from you?

Choosing a Corn Snake

Before anything, you must first check the snake for any signs of health problems. In your hands, it should feel smooth and firm but without any soft spots. Check the anal vent – there should be no signs of discharge. Its nostrils must be clear with no moisture and the mouth should close with no problem. Your snake shouldn't have any breathing problems. You should also check the snake for any injuries. Try handling it carefully and examining it – with supervision, of course!

Make sure to ask the seller if the corn snake has eaten. If it hasn't, don't buy it – some hatchlings end up starving themselves to death. Ask if the snake is used to eating live or frozen mice.

Your corn snake shouldn't have trouble calming down once it is picked up. It should be able to move without any problems.

It is always better to choose a corn snake bred in captivity, because wild corn snakes may carry with them health problems and parasites. They are also harder to handle. Corn snakes bred in captivity are easier to handle.

List of Snake Breeders

While going to the local pet shop is convenient, going online to buy your corn snake may save you some money. If you want to see your corn snake up close and personal, however, you may want to opt for local breeders in your area. Go to reptile fairs. Speak to the breeders. Try looking for reptile or corn snake groups. The people in these groups are usually knowledgeable about reptiles and snakes, and may give you good advice on where to get your corn snake. You can also try visiting corn snake forums to ask for advice.

Below is a list of some of the different websites where you can get your corn snake. We have also listed some forums discussing corn snakes:

U.S. and U.K. Snake Sellers and Breeders:

VMSherp.com
<http://www.vmsherp.com/LCBreedingCorns.htm>

Back Water Reptiles
<http://www.backwaterreptiles.com/corn-snakes-for-sale.html>

BHB Reptiles
<https://www.bhbreptiles.com/collections/corn-snakes>

Helpful Groups and Forums:

The Corn Snake Forum
<http://www.thecornsnake.co.uk/forum/>

Cornsnakes.com
<http://www.cornsnakes.com/forums/>

Fauna Classifieds
<http://www.faunaclassifieds.com/forums/forumdisplay.php?f=501>

Ian's Vivarium
<http://iansvivarium.com/forum/>

Reptile Forums UK
<http://www.reptileforums.co.uk/>

Still, the best way to ensure you get a healthy snake is by seeing it up close and personal, so it is highly suggested going to reptile fairs and meeting other people with the same interest in corn snakes. You'll learn a lot, sure, but you may also will make a friend, or maybe meet your soul mate!

Chapter Four: Maintenance for Your Corn Snake

Having a pet snake is something different and sometimes, maintenance can be a struggle. It truly comes with a great deal of responsibility. If you happen to decide to buy your own Corn Snake, you have to be sure that you can provide their necessities so that it will stay healthy and happy. This chapter will give you basic information in maintaining a Corn Snake including tips on setting up their enclosure, a complete guide in taking care of them and ways on how to keep your Corn Snake s happy.

Building and Maintaining Your Corn Snake's Home

Caging

In the wild, corn snakes prefer staying in overgrown fields, forest openings, trees, and even abandoned buildings and farms. This gives them plenty of room and space to hide as they live near their prey – rodents. If you want to own a corn snake, you must first consider if you have the capacity to build and maintain a good home for your soon-to-be pet.

Baby corn snakes can live in a small plastic vivarium the size of a large shoebox. However, when they grow into adults they need a 20-gallon long aquarium at the very least. Check if you have that much space in your home before anything else.

Make sure to provide some dark hiding spaces for your snake to help them feel secure, and some branches for them to climb. Fill the tank with plants and boxes to hide in. Snakes may get traumatized when they can't hide, so give them room and accessories to feel secure. Privacy is as important to a snake as it is to us. Use rocks and treated wood available in pet stores.

Only one corn snake should stay in a cage as they get stressed easily. While they are docile, they are not exactly friendly to other animals. Make sure that their cages are inescapable, as snakes with their long bodies can easily get through small openings. Not exercising caution and failing to check the cage will not end well for both you and your corn snake. It is best to use a mesh lid so the tank will have enough ventilation.

Lighting and Temperature

Natural light from windows will let your corn snake adjust its day and night cycles as well as its seasonal cycles. However, be careful to keep their cage away from direct sunlight as the temperature may become lethal for your corn snake.

Use a temperature gradient with a light or under tank heat pad or cable. Your snake tank should have a warm zone and a cool zone, with a hiding area in each zone. 85 degrees Fahrenheit is a good warm temperature while around 70 degrees Fahrenheit is a good cool temperature. While your local pet shop may suggest getting heat rocks, using heat rocks is not recommended. Snakes have sensitive skin and are prone to burns.

Use a long, skinny hiding place for your snake: a hollow log or PVC pipe. Keep one end cool and the other end warm. This keeps the temperature at a comfortable level for your corn snake. When checking the temperature, check inside the warm end of the hide and not on the glass as the temperature may be different.

Increase the humidity inside the hide box by adding a clump of damp moss or paper towel if your snake prepares to shed. Remember to remove it between sheds to avoid having unwanted bacteria, mold, and more.

Bedding

Breeders often use aspen shavings because it is absorbent, soft, and it holds its shape when snakes burrow. You may also use Cypress mulch, but avoid aromatic woods like pine or cedar because the oils can be toxic to your corn snake. You can also opt for newspaper and reptile carpet; however, corn snakes get under it when they can. Do not use 'reptile sand' – it may cause impactions your snake ingests it.

Cleaning

At the very least, one must do a thorough cage cleaning once a month to keep the cage free from bacteria which may be harmful to your corn snake. Besides doing full cleanings, you must also spot clean the cage when you have to – cleaning the water bowls weekly, removing feces and shed skin, and more.

Before doing a full cleanse of your corn snake's cage, you must first find a suitable temporary cage for your snake. Check for components you need to clean and replace such as the bedding of the cage. After doing these, you may start cleaning by following these steps:

- Gather your cleaning materials. Paper towels, spray disinfectant, water sprayer, trash bag, and other materials you think will come in handy.
- Relocate your corn snake to a temporary cage. A medium-sized Rubbermaid box with a lockable lid and air holes will do.
- Remove all the cage furniture items and decorations such as bowls, hides, branches, rocks, plants, and place them in the bathtub or sink.
- Unplug all the electrical devices on the cage such as heating and lighting.
- Remove old substrate. If your bedding of choice is shavings or something similar, dump the cage or use a vacuum.
- Clean the empty cage. Use a spray bottle with water and paper towels to clear the dust, feces, and other dirt. Afterwards, use an antibacterial disinfectant.
- Leave the cage open so it can finish drying completely while you clean the other items.
- Clean the cage items with antibacterial soap and hot water. You may soak some items overnight in

a diluted bleach solution (One part bleach to four parts water) if you have difficulty getting the dirt out.

- Make sure to clean the water bowl thoroughly with antibacterial soap and hot water. Rinse with hot water.
- Do not scrub plastic bowls with fingernails or scouring pads. It will leave scratches on the bowl and it will make it harder to clean in the future. Instead, use the smooth part of your finger to rub the bowl clean, or soak it overnight.
- Add new bedding and replace the cage furniture. Fill up the bowl with fresh water.
- Put your snake back in and plug in the electrical devices. Make sure all the locks and latches are secure.

Caring Tips for Your Corn Snake

- Put your snakes alone in its terrarium or with appropriate buddies.

- Feed your snakes alone to avoid food aggression.

- Be sure to stay away from your snake until the lump from the prey disappears. Don't carry your snake up until it has digested the prey enough that the lump in its middle has disappeared, because it might still feel aggressive before its food is digested

- Provide fresh water. Use a relatively deep bowl, check the water bowl every day and always keep it clean. If the Corn Snake starts to feel very moist, take the water bowl out and return it for a few days every week.

- Handle your snake gently. Keep in mind that this is a wild animal, so it may be afraid of you for quite some time. Gently hold your snake and stay away from its face, especially at first.

- Watch for shedding. Never handle your snake when you think it's getting ready to shed. It will be obvious that this is happening when their skin starts to turn milky or bluish. In just a few days, they'll crawl completely out of their old skin, and by then, it will be safe to hold them again.

- Don't restrain your snake. Corn Snakes almost never bite, but if you restrain them, they may. Never pinch or squeeze them. Let them flow gently through your hands and fingers.

Common Maintenance Problems

- Find a vet who is expert about snakes. You may have to travel to find a competent vet since most vets don't come in contact with snakes that often that is why it is a great idea to get connected with one before anything goes wrong.

- Watch for mites. Mites love to live on Corn Snakes. Keep an eye out especially around their mouth, eyes, and under their scales. If ever your snake becomes lethargic or not eating, this might be caused by mites so always give them an inspection.

- Keep an eye out for respiratory infections. If your Corn Snakes sounds wheezy or experience excessive saliva, it may have a respiratory infection that may be caused by a dirty cage, low temperatures, or contact with another infected snake. In some cases, Corn Snakes will need an antibiotic so it's better to consult your vets.

- Pay attention to regurgitation. It's not unusual for Corn Snakes to regurgitate after eating but since this may be a sign of serious illness, you should keep an eye on your Corn Snake for other symptoms if you see them do this. If it happens most of the times, and your snake starts to lose weight, do not hesitate to take it to the vet.

Ways to Keep your Corn Snake Happy

- Make sure your snake's vivarium is of a suitable size
- Correct vivarium temperature
- Maintain scrupulous hygiene
- Provide environmental enrichment
- Handle your Corn Snake regularly & carefully
- Avoid stressing them out

Maintaining Humidity

A Corn Snake enclosure should be kept at 40 - 50 percent humidity. If the humidity is extremely low, a daily misting will provide the higher humidity that aids in proper shedding. Corn Snake should not be kept in a damp environment since this can lead to skin infections and other problems in your pet.

Useful Tools and Devices

As long as the basic requirement for a proper habitat is met, taking care of your Corn Snake will get relatively easier. The trickiest part would be keeping the temperature and humidity at their proper levels, but once that's done, you won't have to think too much about other details. Fortunately enough, there are a number of devices and gadgets that can help you monitor these pertinent environmental factors. Using these, you can make sure that your Corn Snake's habitat is the closest it can be to its natural requirements. A mistake in any of these – light, heat, or humidity – can cause various problems in your pet such as illnesses or diseases, behavioral changes, and sometimes even death – such as if temperature rises too high and causes them to dry out.

Some of the tools or gadgets you should perhaps invest in and familiarize yourself with include:

- A simple light timer to automate the on/off cycles of your light sources
- A thermometer to help you measure the heat and temperature
- A thermostat to help you in regulating the temperature by turning heating sources on and off as needed
- A rheostat can act as a dimmer, reducing or increasing the amount of power that goes to a certain device such as a light or heat source
- A hygrometer to help you monitor the humidity levels

Chapter Five: Nutritional Needs of Corn Snakes

While feeding your Corn Snake might seem strange and difficult, it is actually fairly simple. You have to take in mind that snakes are predators and meat-eaters, so you have to see how comfortable you are with feeding animals to your snake before actually getting one as a pet. Corn Snake covers a broad spectrum of dietary requirements and it is very important to note that they maintain some degree of carnivore throughout their lifecycle. They should be consuming appropriate-sized prey for proper nutrition - that is the basic fact that you need to know in owning a

Corn Snake. If you want a healthy snake, you should strive hard to give its proper nutrition and keep it that way. This section will illustrate and explain how to properly feed your Corn Snake and their nutritional needs that they need to meet in order to maintain a healthy lifestyle.

Feeding Guidelines Your Corn Snake

In the wild, Corn Snakes will eat any bird or animal small enough to be swallowed whole. These include rats, rodents etc. While in captivity, they should be fed rodents, usually mice which are easy to get because of its availability. You can offer live or well-thawed frozen mice to them but you should think twice of feeding them live adult mice because they can inflict wounds to your Corn Snakes. Fresh killed mice are the best choice.

Although Corn Snakes prefer to eat rodents such as mice, especially in captivity, there are also a wide variety of choices which you can feed them. These are the following food choices, including those that they eat in the wild and some guidelines on how to feed them:

As mentioned earlier, wild corn snakes feed on rodents. However, since rodents may be too big for baby corn snakes, they eat lizards and frogs before growing big enough to eat rats. Adult corn snakes also eat birds and their eggs.

Rodents, Rats and Mice

For your pet corn snake, you may buy frozen mice to thaw and feed your snake. Adult corn snakes learn to eat previously frozen and thawed out mice but baby corn snakes have to get used to it. Be prepared to feed baby corn snakes live newborn mice before they get used to eating thawed out mice.

To get your corn snake to focus on its food, you can place it next to a thawed mouse in an empty container with air holes and closing the lid. Cut into the skin of a thawed mouse to ensure faster digestion. Baby corn snakes feed once every five to seven days while adult corn snakes feed once every seven to ten days.

Corn snakes are constrictor snakes. They catch their prey and squeeze it. If you are feeding your snake thawed rodents, you may want to give it the feeling of catching its own food. Defrost the mouse and let it warm to room temperature before holding it by the tail with feeding forceps. Dangle the mouse in front of your snake so it can grab it and swallow the mouse. Occasionally, you may also feed your snake quail eggs.

Make sure to leave some fresh, clean water in a container for your snake and change it regularly.

Bird Eggs

Corn Snakes are well-known for eating eggs of some bird species. Besides the fact that eggs are easily sneaked from a bird's nest, it is also a good source of protein for your snake.

Small Birds and Fish

In the wild, Corn Snakes do not need to worry about chasing a bird away from its nest. Corn Snakes are large enough to ingest a small bird then it will eventually kill the parents and then eat its eggs. Baby birds are an easy meal for Corn Snakes (or any other snakes for that matter). They also eat a variety of fish, ranging from small minnows up to large bass.

Small Lizards

As mentioned earlier, Corn Snakes feed on other snakes and they are perhaps most famous for that habit. They are also known to eat lizards while they are still young.

Frogs

Baby Corn Snakes also eat frogs but keep in mind that feeding frogs to Corn Snakes in captive puts it at risk, some frogs are poisonous or has diseases make sure to check them first.

Promoting Proper Eating Habits for Corn Snakes

The first thing you need to consider to make sure that your Corn Snakes eats properly is to maintain and set up its habitat correctly. Corn Snakes have its own unique habitat requirements referring to lighting, temperature, humidity, layout, accessories, size of the habitat, and more. A Corn Snakes that is in an environment that is too dark, too cold, too small, or else improperly maintained will most probably have a decrease in appetite and may eventually refuse food completely. Be sure to set up and stabilize their habitat before bringing your Corn Snakes home, and also monitor it with thermometers, timers, hygrometers, and other helpful equipment.

Using a Separate Feeding Enclosure

In feeding your Corn Snakes, a separate feeding enclosure may not be a requirement in some cases, but it can definitely be helpful. Using a different environment for feeding times can maintain the main enclosure cleaner and more sanitary. A separate feeding enclosure is recommended if you are housing more than one Corn Snakes in a habitat, to prevent them from viewing other snakes as prey, and if you utilize a substrate that can be ingested.

Corn Snake Feeding Schedule

The time of day when feeding your Corn Snakes depends on what time he is most active. Some species of Corn Snakes are nocturnal, therefore should be fed at night.

How often you feed your Corn Snakes depends on what species he is as well as how old he is. Baby Corn Snakes won't actually start looking for prey until they are two to four weeks old. Generally, your young snakes need to eat about once every week or so, or depending on how quickly you want them to grow. As your Corn Snake gets older, it will not need to be fed as much. Adult Corn Snakes should be fed once or twice a week.

Pre-Killed vs. Live

Many people who own snakes insist that their pets need the thrill of hunting and catching live prey, such as mice and rats. This is definitely not true. Physical and mental stimulation comes from the overall environment that you create for your Corn Snake, and not from attempting to catch a live prey in a small space.

It is recommended to feed your Corn Snake pre-killed prey for a number of reasons. Check out the following:

- Live preys can be too active for your baby Corn Snakes

- Attacks that come from live prey can permanently scar and disfigure your Corn Snake.

- There is a large possibility that live prey can attack your Corn Snake, which results to become frightened of it, and it can be very difficult to get that snake to feed him from them on.

- Live prey can fight back during feeding your Corn Snake, causing injuries such as biting through your snake's mouth area, cutting through its tongue's health, and puncturing his eyes.

Therefore, feeding your snake a pre-killed prey is safer, and it will set aside the possibility that the prey may bite and gnaw your snake. What kind of prey you're feeding your Corn Snake will determine how serious an attack it can potentially cause.

If you like to feed your Corn Snakes a live prey, it is recommended that you provide a food source for the prey so it will not try to eat your snake. You have to watch it closely for any signs that it may be gnawing or biting your snake. If ever this will happen, remove the prey immediately and take your Corn Snake to the veterinarian.

Remember, the threats that a live prey animal present can be completely eliminated by just feeding pre-killed prey instead. Pre-killed prey can be bought live and then you can just kill it, or you can buy it already killed. You can freeze pre-killed prey for up to six months. Just be sure to thaw it thoroughly and warm it to slightly above room temperature before feeding it to your Corn Snake.

Tips for Feeding Pre-Killed Prey to your Corn Snakes

Your Corn Snake might take immediately to pre-killed prey but if your snake is a little bit picky, the following tips might be helpful:

- Rub the live prey that your Corn Snake prefers against the pre-killed prey before putting in in the terrarium

- Prepare a dish of warm chicken broth and dip the pre-killed prey there.

- Use hemostats or tongs to dangle the prey and "walk" it around the enclosure to make it appear as if the prey is alive and attract the snake to strike at it.

- Make sure that the prey is warmer compared to the room temperature because in that way, it will smell more appetizing to your snake.
- Pierce the braincase of the prey with a nail or a pin to release more appetizing odors.

- Feed your Corn Snake a different colored prey. For example, if you've already tried a white mouse, try switching to a brown mouse instead.

Feeding a Corn Snake can be quite hard at first, but with little effort, time, and the right methods at your fingertips, you can keep you snake happy, healthy, and well-nourished.

Corn Snake's Diet

- Avoid feeding your Corn Snake wild-caught prey because this can transmit parasites to the snake. The best option is to offer thawed/ frozen rodents, since the freezing process kills any potential parasites the rodents may have.

- You do not need to supplement your Corn Snake's meals with vitamin powders or similar products. Corn Snake can get all the vitamins and minerals that they need from the food that you feed them, without the need to add anything

- As mentioned above, supplements are not necessary for your Corn Snake unless your snake has certain medical needs.

- You should always take note that fresh water in a shallow dish must always be available.

- Corn Snake aren't picky eaters, so many of them will live their whole lives eating nothing but mice.

- Take into account of using tongs when feeding your Corn Snake to avoid accidental bites.

- When preparing a pre-killed prey for your pet, thaw it by running it under warm water or setting it in the sun so be sure not to sit it for too long as harmful bacteria can start to form on it.

- Baby Corn Snake do well eating only one pinky mouse once every week or so.

- Increase the size of the rodent appropriately as your snake grows. A recommended sized meal is one that is no bigger than the width of the snake's body, or leaves only a small lump in the snake's body after being consumed; anything that is too large will result in regurgitation, injuries, seizures, partial paralysis, gut impactions, and death.

- As soon as your Corn Snake has reached its adult length, you can feed it 1-2 large adult mice every one to two weeks.

- Always remember to feed your snake its prey animals one at a time only and never leave them with live prey unattended for so long especially when your Corn Snake is not hungry as mouse has the tendency to claw, scratch, and bite your snake.

- Be aware that your Corn Snake can get injured or can sometimes die from prey injuries and bites.

Chapter Six: Corn Snake Husbandry

Husbandry simply means the regular and daily care of a pet snake. Two of the most important facets of snake husbandry have already been discussed in the previous chapters: housing and feeding.

In this chapter, we take a look at some of the other aspects types of husbandry care and maintenance that you will need to do to make sure that your Corn Snake is kept clean, safe, and in good health.

Cleaning and Disinfecting the Snake Cage and Habitat

Aside from providing appropriate heating, lighting, humidity, and cage structures and décor, you will also want to clean your Corn Snake's habitat enclosure regularly. This is particularly important as the prevailing humidity within the enclosure can be a perfect ground for the growth of bacteria. Most reptiles can be prone to skin and bacterial infection if left alone in unclean surroundings for long.

Regular cage maintenance and cleaning should be part of your routine. Not only will this keep the interior of the enclosure clean, odor-free, and healthy, but it will also keep you and your family safe and healthy. Regular cleaning prevents the possible transmission of diseases like Salmonella, which can be found in the fecal matter of reptiles, and which may be transmissible to humans.

Spot cleaning the interior of the cage should be done as often as possible – at least once a day, or once every other day. Spot cleaning your reptile's cage can include:

- The removal of fecal matter as soon as you notice them
- The removal of shed skin
- The removal of uneaten food
- Cleaning and refilling the water bowls at least twice a week

A more thorough cage cleaning should be done at least once a month, ideally more. During this process, you will need to relocate the snake so that you can clean and sterilize the entire cage components, including perches, decorations, substrate, etc. To be able to do this thoroughly, you will need to temporarily relocate your Corn Snake to a different holding cage or cell. As usual, make sure that this cage is secure and clean, and is sufficiently ventilated.

- **Remove all of the cage items, disposing directly of the substrate which you will be replacing completely.**

Set aside these cage items in a bowl or container. You will now proceed to clean the inside of the terrarium or cage, and then later on to disinfect and sterilize the cage items. Gather the following materials to help you in your cleaning tasks:

- A spray bottle
- Brushes, Q-tips, putty knives, or razor blades
- Buckets
- Terrarium cleaner that is safe for reptiles
- Paper towels
- Robber gloves
- Sponges

- **Learn to unplug everything!**

Make sure that all the electrical components of the cage – such as heating and lighting, are turned off or unplugged. Then armed with a spray bottle, a sponge, gloves, and just regular soap and water, begin to clean the interior of the snake cage as thoroughly as possible. Make use of instruments such as brushes, Q-tips, putty knives, or razor blades to really get at the hardened feces or waste that a regular paper towel won't be able to dislodge. Really get into it, using herp-safe terrarium cleaners for the really troublesome spots and corners. Rinse the inside of the cage thoroughly.

- **Clean and disinfect the cage items by boiling them in water for some 30 minutes.**

The only way to be sure is to kill any thriving bacteria through high heat and boiling temperatures as you thoroughly sterilize each cage item. Try to avoid using regular household chemical cleaners which may prove toxic or harmful to your pet. Besides, even using these types of cleansers cannot really guarantee the thorough elimination of bacteria.

Use a disinfectant to give another through cleaning to all the cage items, including the interior of the snake cage. Then use hot water to rinse of all chemical residues. Allow it all to air-dry, making sure that the cage interior and all the various cage items and implements are thoroughly dried.

- **Reinstall cage items inside**

After doing the steps above, reinstall all the cage items and decorations, this time putting on a new layer of fresh substrate. You might also want to give your Corn Snake a bath before allowing it to return to its newly cleaned and dry terrarium.

Wash and disinfect all your cleaning tools and equipment with the same thoroughness that you practiced when you were cleaning the cage interior and the cage items. And finally, wash your hands thoroughly – using hot, soapy water. Don't forget to finish off with a disinfectant, too.

Tips for Bathing a Corn Snake

Bathing a pet snake is a simple and straightforward process – but with loads of benefits for your pet. An occasional bath for your Corn Snake can therefore go a long way to having a happy and healthy snake. Bathing can help relieve constipation in your snake, and it can also kill mites and promotes shedding.

Use warm spring or filtered water. Don't use tap or chlorinated water as the chemicals in the water can actually irritate their skin. A good range between 100 and 105 degrees Fahrenheit is a good level for a snake bath. And because they are sensitive to temperature changes, you'll want to provide them with a reasonably warm bath.

You can help your snake get into the bath, but more often than not, they will quickly bathe themselves. You don't want your Corn Snake getting away from you during bathing time; you might want to place a sufficiently roomy bowl of the warm bath water in an enclosure.

Just let your Corn Snake swim freely around in the water. If it shows signs of agitation, take it out immediately. Otherwise, let it soak around for 5 to 15 minutes. When it is done, pick it up, gently use a towel to dry it off, and then return it to his now clean, sterilized, disinfected, and thoroughly dried habitat.

Some recommend placing your snake in a holding cage immediately after a bath as some snakes can defecate immediately after a bath, and you don't want him doing this too soon within the newly cleaned cage. Give your Corn Snake sufficient time in the holding cage to do his business before moving him back to his home.

Chapter Seven: Breeding and Raising Corn Snakes

If you find that you actually want to breed corn snakes, keep in mind that there is much more you need to know besides the basics of taking care of a growing corn snake.

In this chapter, we will discuss how to breed and raise your corn snakes to keep or sell. Who knows, you may get someone else to start liking corn snakes too!

Sexing

A successful breeding program begins with a healthy breeding pair. Females usually reach sexual maturity after 31 months, while the sexual maturity of males occurs after 18 months. The process by which you can identify whether a snake is a male or a female is called sexing.

Sexing can be done in either one of two ways: by cloacal popping or cloacal probing. Please take note that you should never sex hatchlings. They are very sensitive and delicate at this stage, and attempting to sex them can injure them severely.

Cloacal popping is done by applying pressure with the thumb just below the vent. This will cause the hemipenes of a male to avert, one on each side of the cloacal opening. Females, on the other hand, may avert her cloaca and erect her scent gland papillae.

Cloacal probing is the more commonly employed means of sexing. It is done by gently inserting a lubricated probe – a slender stainless steel – into the side of the vent, and then sliding them into the pockets that are found on either side of the tail. For males, the probe will slide to a depth of approximately 10 scales, while for a female; it will go for only 3 or 4 scales. Sometimes the probe will only go somewhere between these two ranges, and these are often classified as unsexed snakes. Probing isn't always definitive or certain, and other factors may influence the result such as the pressure you exert on the probe, or something blocking the pockets so you could not insert the probe deep enough. It is essential that you don't try to attempt to probe your snake if you do not have sufficient experience with sexing. A mistake here can injure and damage your snake, and there is always the chance that the results of your probe can be wrong.

More often than not, a determination of a snake's sex can be established from their behavior. Males are generally more active than females. They also tend to refuse food during breeding time. But perhaps the best sign that your snake is a male is when he averts his hemipenes when he is defecating. When he sheds his skin, the hemipenes can be identified as two dried bits of skin at the vent – but which should not be confused with a small bump that can also show in the shed skin of females. Their tail shape can also differ, with the male's being more parallel and bulbous, as opposed to the female's tail which is more tapered in shape.

For a breeding pair, females should ideally be bigger and weightier than males. This is to allow them to have sufficient body weight that can undergo the stress of egg production. Females are usually paired only after they have reached 1,200 to 1,500 grams, which they can reach around the age of 3 or 4 years. Males, on the other hand, can be a lot younger and lighter; some use males that have reached 50 to

700 grams. The selected breeding pair must both be in good health, with good body weight and muscle tone.

Brumation

Brumation is the term called for the cooling period that takes place in order to successfully breed Corn Snakes. The first thing to do to breed Corn Snakes is to start increasing their feeding pattern in late April in order to give your snake an extra fat reserves that they will be needing during brumation. Keep your heaters on in the month of May but cease feeding the snakes for at least 2-3 weeks before you cool them down so that the Corn Snakes can empty their digestive tracks. During brumation, any food leftover will rot in your Corn Snake's stomach which then leads to a deadly infection.

During the month of June, you have to drop your Corn Snake's cage temperatures from 50 to 68 degrees Celsius in a span of 2-3 months. The brumation temperatures can be slightly higher or lower than this. Around early September, you can now begin to slowly return back your Corn Snake's summer temperature. Never heat your Corn Snakes up to quickly because this can affect your male snake's fertility.

Mating

Shedding of female Corn Snake will take place two weeks after they come out of brumation. This is called the post-brumation shed which shows that your female Corn Snake is ready to mate. Introduce your male Corn Snake into the female Corn Snake terrarium. If the female is receptive, mating behavior will start immediately and the male Corn Snake will mate with the female one very soon. Mating can last for a few minutes to a few hours.

Be sure to separate the two Corn Snake after they finished mating because they can be cannibalistic. To increase the chance of fertile eggs, allow your Corn Snakes to mate more than once.

Breeding

You can start breeding your corn snake when it turns a year old, but it would be better to wait until they are 2 or 3 years old before you start. To ensure successful reproduction, your snake may need to cool down or hibernate depending on the geographic origin.

Keep the vivarium at 50 to 68 degrees for 8-12 weeks without food to induce mating behavior once you return it at the normal temperature.

Make sure to keep groups of male and female snakes apart during the year and bring them together for breeding for mating success. Single male-female pairs are also productive.

Females would usually lay 8 to 26 eggs between March and June. Some may also lie again in late summer.

Breeding Groups

For a basic breeding group, it is recommended to purchase two male Corn Snake and four female Corn Snake, as unrelated as possible, unless there is a certain genetic trait that you want to isolate and work with. If they all grow to maturity, you will be having two trios. When the time comes that you need to sell or pick for future generations of breeders, you can mix from the two unrelated trios. If ever something happened to your first male, your second male can breed to all four females. On the other hand, if one female "goes down" you still are in production.

Make sure that the Corn Snake are sexed correctly. You can check it by yourself, or you can have the breeder confirm the sex and show you how. There is a usual mistake that a male is wrongly categorized as female because the hemipenes do not "pop" when checked. You can always double check with a probe. I guess you do not want to raise your snakes in a long period of time only to find out some females are males.

Checking for Sperm and Follicles

You can use a microscope to check for sperm. Take the seminal plug on a mount, add some saline solution if needed (solution used for contact lens also works), and put it under a microscope on shaded screen a 200 power. By then, you have to see a lot of sperm swimming. If not, you may want to use your second male.

Sometimes, it is preferred to use a Calci-Sand because you can see the seminal plug on the sand if your miss the actual mating. In that case, you can gently squeeze a little fluid from the mated female Corn Snake and have a sperm check. You can find a few live sperm up to a week after confirmed mating, but the sooner you test, the better.

Usually, when a female Corn Snake is ready to breed, you can touch and feel her follicles. You can gently indent your thumb up into their rib cage about mid-body, and just let the snake crawl over your thumb. In this way, you can feel bumps like soft marbles. These are the ones that are developed into eggs when fertilized.

Taking Care of a Pregnant Snake

Number one thing we need to do if we have a pregnant snake is that we should observe privacy. Snakes are very, very shy and in times like that, it's a great idea to observe them from afar. Our pet Corn Snake will lay eggs so it's very important that there will be an incubation area and a laying area which is very easy to do. You can use sphagnum moss, peat moss, vermiculite, and what they will just do is they will burrow down in the vermiculite. You have to take note that the substrate should stay moist but not wet. You'll get hatchlings quicker at higher temperatures but you will also get more congenital defects. Those defects normally show up not only in immune problems, but in different patterns of color.

Raising Young Corn Snakes

Keep artificial incubation for baby corn snakes at 82 degrees and 60% humidity for an 80 to 100% hatch rate after 55 to 75 days. Upon hatching, the baby corn snakes will measure 20 to 28 centimeters and will eat pink mice after their first shed, within 3 to 7 days of hatching.

Caring for baby corn snakes is the same as for adults, but you must also pay close attention to keep them from escaping. You must also feed them smaller mice more frequently. Start with pink mice, then small fluffy mice. As the corn snake gets bigger, feed them larger mice until they can finally eat adult mice.

The success rate for breeding corn snakes is high, as it has resulted in self-sustaining captive populations in Europe and North America. Because of this, the cost of corn snakes has gone down. Of course, those with unique-colored variants are highly prized.

Chapter Eight: Training and Taming Your Corn Snake

Corn Snake can be great pets for those who take time to learn on how to properly take care of them. This chapter will give you a whole lot of tips on to be a great owner of a Corn Snake including points on how to properly tame them, handle them, and introduce them to people or other house pets as well. These things are essential in making your pet's lifestyle as fun and wonderful as it can be. It'll make you a better owner if you know your snake's strength and weaknesses.

Getting Along With Your Snake

Hatchling corn snakes are nervous and defensive. It is normal for them to hide or defend themselves, but they cannot really harm you. In fact, an overly excited cat can hurt you more than the largest corn snake!

Give your new pet a few weeks to settle into its home and get used to a regular feeding routine. Remember, snakes are also living beings that need to settle and get used to new spaces. Your snake may take some time getting used to you, so try not to stress it out with unnecessary handling.

After three or four successful meals and when you see that your pet has started getting used to its surroundings, you can start approaching your snake. Start handling it for short periods. However, do not handle it for the first two to three days after a meal.

Approach your corn snake from the side to avoid threatening it as a predator would approach it from the top. Gently but confidently lift it. Hesitation will scare your corn snake and will cause it to hide or bite. Use lightweight cotton gloves as long as you feel it is needed.

When your corn snake realizes you are not going to eat it, it will calm down and tame quickly. Eventually, it will become used to handling.

Tips on How to Tame your Corn Snake

- When you get your new Corn Snake, just leave it for about five days or weeks or so that it can get used to its surroundings because when you get a new snake, it's going to be a little bit feisty. They won't feel like it's a high more secure surrounding.

- Make sure that you give your Corn Snake a plenty of hides because if it's out and if you'll give them a lot of space, it's not going to feel safe for them because in the wild, they will go hide under the rocks, bushes, or wherever.

- If you feed your Corn Snake, don't handle it for at least 24 hours after feeding the snake. Give them time to digest their food because it is not a good idea if you handle it straight after you feed it.

- When you feed your Corn Snake, feed it out of its enclosure so that when the owner put his hand on the snake's cage, it won't think that the hand is a food; thus, preventing to be bitten by your snake.

- Another top tip when you want to handle and tame your Corn Snake is to just put and leave your hand on its cage so it gets used to your hand. In that way, your Corn Snake will know that your hand is not food and won't try to hurt you.

Introducing Yourself to your Corn Snake

Give your Corn Snake time to adjust to you

Whether it's a hatchling or captive-bred Corn Snake might show a little aggression, or with a great deal of aggressive behavior, the first thing you should consider is to allow your Corn Snake to adjust to you. Let's say, for the first week or so, just sit outside its terrarium for about an hour each day and allow it to get used to your smell. Never attempt to touch your Corn Snake during these first few weeks.

Move items around in its terrarium without touching it

At the end of this initial week, you can now begin to move things around inside your Corn Snake's terrarium. However, it is still not allowed to attempt to touch your Corn Snake at this point. Continuously do this for another week so that your Corn Snake can get used to the idea that you have no intention to harm him. Being around it without attempting to touch it will let your Corn Snake know that you are not a danger or threat.

Touch your snake inside its cage

Once you think that your snake know that you are not a threat, you can start to touch it while inside its cage by placing your hand in its cage and gently start touching it, moving it around inside the cage, and lifting your snake's tail. Continue doing this manner to your snake for three to four days.

Dealing with your Corn Snake's Potential Aggression

Determine why it is aggressive

Unless you're taming a Corn Snake hatchling or captive-bred Corn Snake, you'll likely have to deprogram your snake's aggressive behavior. The first thing to do is to know what type of aggression your Corn Snake is showing. There are two types of aggressive responses you can deprogram your Corn Snake – territorial, or defensive responses, and feeding responses.

- Territorial responses are instinctive and not an expression of aggressions. Snakes live most of their lives in fear of being eaten by bigger predators, including humans, so this kind of response is more of a defense mechanism which can be tamed with gentle and consistent care.

- Feeding responses, on the other hand, are also natural, instinctive response. Generally, snakes are taught to bite whatever comes into their terrarium. Since they assume that anything that comes to their cage is food, you might get bitten if you put your hand inside without first deprogramming this aggressive response.

"Hook Train" aggressive Corn Snakes

Some species of Corn Snakes are more aggressive than others and might be requiring more training. If you're dealing with a particularly aggressive type of Corn Snake, you might consider to "hook train" it. You can do this by gently rubbing its body or pushing down on its head with a hook, or a similar inanimate object, every time you go to get it out of its cage. By doing this, your Corn Snake will be able to know it is not yet feeding time so there is no need to bite whatever enters its terrarium.

- If your Corn Snake appears to be scared whenever you open its terrarium, spend a little more time rubbing its body with the hook until it will calm down. For example, if your snake coils into a ball, flattens out its body, or pose a striking position, spend some time rubbing its body until it will come to a point that it will relax a bit.

- Start rubbing your Corn Snake's body down from its tail end and up to its head. It could seem threatening if you start it with its head especially if your snake is already scared.

Hold your snake more often than you feed it

The very most common reason why people get bitten by their pet snake is because their snake is reacting to its feeding response every time something enters its terrarium. To handle this kind of response, stop feeding your Corn Snake every week. Instead, feed it only once every three weeks, but be sure to handle your snake every day. This will deprogram your Corn Snake from thinking that everything that enters its terrarium is food.

- It can also be useful to feed your snake in a separate tub. This will also help it from thinking that everything that comes to its terrarium is food. But don't feed it only in the tub because this will just transfer its response from the terrarium to the tub.

- It is safe to only feed your Corn Snake once every three weeks since Corn Snakes can go weeks without eating, with any harm done.

Handling your Corn Snake Properly

- **Be confident**

After introducing yourself to your snake, and have worked on handling it, you can now begin to handle your snake outside its cage. It is very vital that you handle your snake with confidence. If you are still fearful or hesitant, your snake will be able to sense it and act the same way.

It is a nice idea to handle your Corn Snake under the supervision of a professional or long-time owner before actually getting one for yourself. This will guarantee that you are comfortable with your Corn Snake when you get it.

- **Wash your hands**

You should always wash your hands thoroughly before handling your Corn Snake. Snakes have an excellent sensory organ so if they smell a scent of prey on your hand, your Corn Snake might mistake your hand for something it should eat! That does not sound good!!

Also, washing your hands before handling your Corn Snake helps prevent any foreign bacteria, germs, or parasites in your pet's environment.

- **Provide support for its body**

It is very vital to support your Corn Snake's body when you are picking or handling it up so that it is comfortable with you and there is no strain put on its body. This is true whether you are picking your Corn Snake up with your hands or with a hook. Keep the first third of your snake's body supported with either the hook or one of your hands, while supporting the back two thirds of your Corn Snake's body with your other arm.

Keep in mind your "hook training" before putting your hands in your Corn Snake's terrarium. Lightly pressing down on your Corn Snake's head with a hook will give the snake an idea that it is not feeding time so there is no need to strike. Never grab your Corn Snake by the end of its tail to pick it up or move it. This can cause serious strain and fear to your Corn Snake.

- **Never restrain its head**

Restraining your Corn Snake's head can make it believe that you are a predator that's trying to hurt the snake. Whenever you handle your Corn Snake, stick to holding it by its body, and avoid holding or restraining its head.

- **Point its head away from you**

Until you know within yourself that you can properly handle your snake, it is a good idea to hold it with its head facing away from you. This will give your Corn Snake a chance to become familiarized to you and the motion of your hands or body without the danger that the experience may turn negative.

Creating the Right Environment for your Corn Snake

- **Get the right cage size**

If your Corn Snake is still irritated after you have introduced yourself and deprogrammed it, there could be something on its environment that makes it upset or sick. If your Corn Snake feels upset because it is too cold or hot, or feels threatened or vulnerable in its environment, it is more likely to lash out. Thus, creating and maintaining a right environment for your pet is imperative to taming it. Getting it a proper cage is the first step in creating the environment of your Corn Snake.

- **Provide proper lighting**

Some Corn Snakes are diurnal snakes, others are nocturnal thus they need a bright white light during the day and very dim lighting during the night. You have to place an incandescent white light above your Corn Snake's terrarium if the room you are keeping your snake in has only dim lighting. In this way, you can give them enough light. On the other hand, they need very little light during the night. Decorative incandescent lights that come in dark colors such as red, blue, and green will give the right amount of light during the night.

Heating and lighting your Corn Snake's cage go hand in hand so you may want to pay attention to how one affects the other

- **Provide a primary heat source**

Corn Snakes require the right temperature to live comfortably. This means they require both a primary and secondary heat source. Primary heat source is needed to keep the temperature of the entire terrarium in the correct range. You can do this by adding a series of incandescent lights along the top of the terrarium.

There are a lot of varieties to create the right night time temperature on your Corn Snake's terrarium. You can use different options such as a heating pad placed under the snake's terrarium, ceramic infrared heat emitters, or nocturnal reptile incandescent light bulbs. All of these things that were mention provide heat without much light

Use several thermometers and place it in your Corn Snake's terrarium to ensure that you are keeping it at optimal temperatures.

- **Provide a secondary heat source**

Snakes need a temperature gradient in their terrariums so that they can go to whichever temperature is most comfortable for them. You can do this by installing a secondary heat source in your Corn Snake's terrarium.

In order to create this secondary heat source, you can either place an under-the tank-heater underneath only one-quarter of the tank or you can mount a 50 to 75 watt incandescent light bulb located on the outside of one wall of the snake's terrarium.

"Basking lights" are a very great choice to create a heat gradient as well. Basking lights are placed outside the terrarium wherein it creates heat in one specific area of the tank.

- **Create various hiding places for your Corn Snake**

Snakes are hiders by nature, especially when they are in the wild. They often hide if they feel threatened so if you do not have places for them to hide, it will likely feel threatened and vulnerable, thus, resulting to a potentially aggressive behavior.

Great hiding places may be a cave made of rock or a clean piece of cardboard. You can also be creative and use plastic or clay flowerpots as their hiding places.

- **Provide water**

Just like any other animals, Corn Snakes need water in order to survive. Be sure that your pet snake has clean and fresh water all the time. You can use a water bowl in its terrarium, but make sure it is not easily tipped over.

Important Reminders:

- Do not handle a Corn Snake if it's shedding because they might be more aggressive during these times.

- You can still expect your Corn Snake to exhibit some defensive behavior even though they are tamed. These behaviors include emitting a foul-smelling odor, musking, thrashing, or biting. However, these actions are not dangerous since Corn Snakes are non-venomous snakes and don't normally cause any serious injury.

Chapter Nine: Keeping Your Corn Snake Healthy

Once you've bought a healthy corn snake, you must know how to keep it healthy. What do they need? How much should you feed them? What are the symptoms of possible diseases? You should be able to tell when your corn snake needs a trip to the vet.

In this chapter, we will talk about what your corn snake needs to stay healthy, and what to look out for when your snake doesn't look like it's at peak condition.

Common Health Problems

Snakes can be affected by a number of different health problems and they are generally not specific to any particular breed. Feeding your Corn Snake a nutritious diet will go a long way in securing his total health and wellbeing, but sometimes snakes get ill anyway. If you want to make sure that your snake gets the treatment he needs as quickly as possible you need to learn how to identify the symptoms of disease. These symptoms are not always obvious either; your Corn Snake may not show any outward signs of illness except for a subtle change in behavior.

The more time you spend with your pet snake, the more you will come to understand his behavior – this is the key to catching health problems early. At the first sign that something is wrong with your snake you should take inventory of his symptoms – both physical and behavioral – so you can relay them to your veterinarian who will then make a diagnosis and prescribe a course of treatment. The sooner you identify these symptoms, the sooner your vet can take action and the more likely your Corn Snake will be able to make a full recovery.

Corn Snake can be prone to a wide variety of different diseases or infections, though some are more common than others. For the benefit your Corn Snake's long-term health, take the time to learn the causes, symptoms, and treatment options for some of the most common health problems.

Besides red flags, it is best to be in the know when it comes to what these red flags mean. Corn snakes have some common health issues you can find by identifying the symptoms or causes. Here are some of the common health issues to look out for:

Dermatitis

- Symptoms: Blisters, rapid shedding.
- Causes: Unclean habitat, temperature and humidity too cold or too damp.
- What to do: Consult your veterinarian, clean habitat and lower humidity.

Respiratory Disease

- Symptoms: Labored breathing, mucus in mouth   and/or nostrils.
- Causes: Habitat too cold or damp.
- What to do: Consult veterinarian, keep snake warm and dry.

Stomatitis

- Symptoms: White, cheesy substance in mouth, loss of teeth and appetite.
- What to do: Fatal when untreated, so consult your veterinarian immediately.

Ticks and mites

- Symptoms: Parasites on skin.
- What to do: Consult your veterinarian.

Checking Your Snake's Health

To be able to tell that something's wrong with your snake, you must first know what a healthy corn snake looks like. Listed below are some signs you can see in a healthy snake:

- **Active**
Your corn snake must be able to move freely at its normal pace.

- **Clear eyes**

One of the first signs of a healthy animal is having clear eyes. Check your corn snake's eyes. Except when shedding, if it's healthy, it will have clear eyes.

- **Regular eating**

Eating is the most basic of needs – if your snake isn't eating when it's supposed to, something's wrong.

- **Healthy skin**

Check your snake's scales during handling. Its body should feel firm enough to the touch but without being too soft.

- **Regularly sheds skin**

When your snake sheds, check if it's shedding in one piece. This means that your snake doesn't have any skin problems and your tank is set at the perfect humidity for your corn snake.

- **Free of parasites**

Your snake should be free of parasites such as mites and ticks.

Once you know what your corn snake should look like when it's in good condition, you will know what red flags to look for. Below are a quick checklist or red flags that you should attend to immediately:

- **Infrequent or irregular shedding**
- **Vomiting**
- **Reluctance to eat**
- **Abnormal feces**
- **Bumps on skin**
- **Difficulty breathing**
- **Difficulty shedding**
- **Substance forming at the mouth**

When you encounter these signs, it's time to take your corn snake for a visit to the vet.

Corn Snake Care Sheet

Congratulate yourself! You are now on your way to becoming a very well-informed and pro-active Corn Snake owner! Finishing this book is a huge milestone for you and your future or present pet, but before this ultimate guide comes to a conclusion, keep in mind the most important things you have acquired through reading this book.

In the previous chapters, we have discussed the characteristics of a corn snake, what it needs, the different tools you will need, the costs of keeping a pet corn snake, how to keep it healthy, and breeding.

It may be a lot of information to take in, so we have compiled a care sheet to summarize the information you can find in this book.

Basic Information

- **Scientific Name:** *Pantherophis guttatus*

- **Breed Size as they hatch from their eggs**: 8 to 12 inches
- **Average size**: 2 to 6 feet
- **Maximum adult size:** 6 feet
- **Caging:** bigger is better
- **Food**: Lizards, rodents, birds.
- **Skin Pattern**: Similar to corn kernels
- **Color**: Yellow, Red, Orange, Black
- **Temperament**: docile and calm
- **Health Conditions**: have no special health requirements aside from normal snake diseases and health concerns
- **Wild Diet:** Feeds on rodents, lizards, and birds.
- **Museum Diet:** Mice and small rats.

- **Life Span in the Wild:** 10 to 20 years
- **Life Span in Captivity:** 15 to 20 years
- **Overall Lifespan:** average 20 to 25 years

Habitat Requirements

- **Recommended Equipment:** Terrarium or snake cage/enclosure, water bowl, substrate, plants, driftwood, moss, and rocks, heat and light sources, thermometer, thermostat, light timer
- **Recommended Day/Light Cycle:** 12-12 hours
- **Recommended Temperature:** 70-85 degrees Fahrenheit
- **Recommended Humidity Levels:** No required humidity level; light misting
- **Cleaning Frequency:** Full cleaning once a month; Regular spot cleaning.

Nutritional Needs

- **Primary Diet:** Mice, Rodents.
- **Feeding Frequency (Hatchlings):** Every five to seven days
- **Feeding Frequency (Adult):** Once every seven to ten days

- **Water:** Fresh water in a bowl should be always available.

Breeding Information

- **Age of Sexual Maturity:** 2-3 years old
- **Number of eggs**: around 26 eggs
- **Recommended Incubation Temperatures:** 82 degrees Fahrenheit
- **Recommended Incubation Humidity Levels:** 60 percent
- **Length at Birth:** 20 to 28 cm

Index

G

H

I

J

K

L

M

N

O

P

Photo Credits

Page 1 Photo by user sipa via Pixabay.com

<https://pixabay.com/en/corn-snake-413072/>

Page 11 Photo by user FraukeFeind via Pixabay.com

<https://pixabay.com/en/corn-snake-snakes-terraristik-606671/>

Page 18 Photo by user sipa via Pixabay.com

<https://pixabay.com/en/snake-natter-corn-snake-reptile-879919/>

Page 32 Photo by user sipa via Pixabay.com

<https://pixabay.com/en/corn-snake-snake-588654/>

Page 46 Photo by user Kapa65 via Pixabay.com

<https://pixabay.com/en/snake-corn-snake-reptile-scale-676335/>

Page 57 by user FeatherWolfGD via Pixabay.com

<https://pixabay.com/en/snakes-corn-yellow-1662401/>

Page 68 Photo by user Kapa65 via Pixabay.com

<https://pixabay.com/en/snake-corn-snake-stone-shoe-749010/>

Page 74 Photo by user FraukeFeind via Pixabay.com

<https://pixabay.com/en/corn-snake-snakes-terraristik-666912/>

Page 84 Photo by user Bartłomiej W (Ozi) via Wikimedia Commons

<https://commons.wikimedia.org/wiki/File:W%C4%85%C5%BC_zbo%C5%BCowy_by_Ozi.jpg>

Page 98 Photo by user Piatkowskk via Wikimedia Commons
<https://commons.wikimedia.org/wiki/File:Zwei_Kornnattern.jpg>

Page 105 Photo by user Linda Tanner via Wikimedia Commons
<https://commons.wikimedia.org/wiki/File:Pantherophis_guttatus_Head.jpg>

References

"Brief Introduction to Corn Snakes" The Corn Snake.co.uk
<http://www.thecornsnake.co.uk/>

"Caring For Your Corn Snake" All About Corn Snakes.com
<http://www.allaboutcornsnakes.com>

"Colubrid: Snake Family" Encyclopedia Britannica
<https://www.britannica.com/animal/colubrid>

"Convincing your family about a pet snake" Pet-Snakes.com
<http://pet-snakes.com/convince-family-pet-snake>

"Corn Snake" Petco.com
<http://www.petco.com/content/petco/PetcoStore/en_US/pet-services/resource-center/caresheets/corn-snake.html>

"Corn Snake" Toledozoo.org

<http://www.toledozoo.org/naturesneighborhood/petcareinfo/PDF/PetGuide-CornSnake_print.pdf>

"Corn Snake Care" By Martin Spicer, Martin's Reptiles

<http://www.martinsreptiles.co.uk/cornsnakecare.htm>

"Corn Snake Care Sheet" The Corn Snake.co.uk

<http://www.thecornsnake.co.uk/corn_snake_care_sheet.htm>

"Corn Snake Care Sheet" by Kathy Love, Reptiles Magazine

<http://www.reptilesmagazine.com/Care-Sheets/Snakes/Corn-Snake/>

"Corn Snakes for Sale" BackwaterReptiles.com

<http://www.backwaterreptiles.com/corn-snakes-for-sale.html>

"Corn Snakes: Morphs, Colors, & Other Facts" by Jessie Szalay, Live Science
<http://www.livescience.com/44008-corn-snakes.html>

"How Do I Choose a Cornsnake?" by user Nghi, YoExpert
<http://exotic-pets.yoexpert.com/reptiles-and-amphibians/how-do-i-choose-a-cornsnake-30516.html>

"How to Breed Corn Snakes" VMSherp.com
<http://www.vmsherp.com/LCBreedingCorns.htm>

"How to Care for a Corn Snake" wikiHow.com
<http://www.wikihow.com/Care-for-a-Corn-Snake>

"How to Clean a Snake Cage Quickly and Easily" Reptile Knowledge
<http://www.reptileknowledge.com/news/how-to-clean-a-snake-cage-quickly-and-easily/>

"Introduction" Corn Snake pictures and facts
<http://fohn.net/corn-snake-pictures-facts/>

"Keeping Corn Snakes as Pets: The Best Choice for You?"
Reptile Knowledge
<http://www.reptileknowledge.com/care/corns-as-pets.php>

"Online Help & Advice for Corn Snake Owners"
Cornsnake.co.uk
<http://www.cornsnake.co.uk/>

"Pantherophis guttatus" Florida Museum, University of
Florida
<http://www.flmnh.ufl.edu/herpetology/fl-
snakes/list/pantherophis-guttatus>

"Pantherophis guttatus" The IUCN Red List of Threatened
Species
<http://www.iucnredlist.org/details/63863/0>

"The real cost of keeping a snake" Pet-Snakes.com
<http://pet-snakes.com/cost-of-keeping-a-snake>

"What does a corn snake eat?" Reptile Knowledge
<http://www.reptileknowledge.com/news/corn-snake-eat-127/ >

"What Do Corn Snakes Eat & How to Care for Them"
petMD.com
<http://www.petmd.com/reptile/care/evr_rp_corn_snake>

Feeding Baby
Cynthia Cherry
978-1941070000

Axolotl
Lolly Brown
978-0989658430

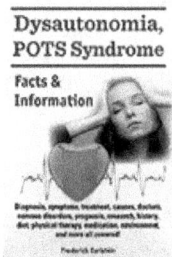

Dysautonomia, POTS
Syndrome
Frederick Earlstein
978-0989658485

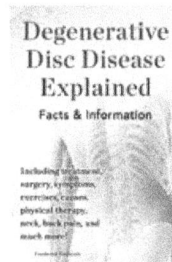

Degenerative Disc
Disease Explained
Frederick Earlstein
978-0989658485

Sinusitis, Hay Fever,
Allergic Rhinitis Explained
Frederick Earlstein
978-1941070024

Wicca
Riley Star
978-1941070130

Zombie Apocalypse
Rex Cutty
978-1941070154

Capybara
Lolly Brown
978-1941070062

Eels As Pets
Lolly Brown
978-1941070167

Scabies and Lice Explained
Frederick Earlstein
978-1941070017

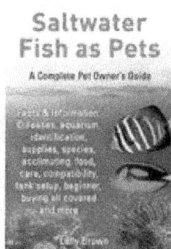

Saltwater Fish As Pets
Lolly Brown
978-0989658461

Torticollis Explained
Frederick Earlstein
978-1941070055

Kennel Cough

Kennel Cough
Lolly Brown
978-0989658409

Physiotherapist, Physical Therapist

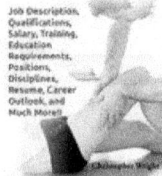

Physiotherapist, Physical Therapist
Christopher Wright
978-0989658492

Rats, Mice, and Dormice As Pets

Rats, Mice, and Dormice As Pets
Lolly Brown
978-1941070079

Wallaby and Wallaroo Care

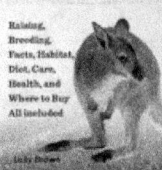

Wallaby and Wallaroo Care
Lolly Brown
978-1941070031

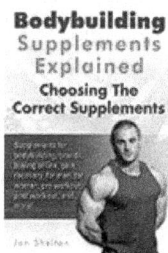

Bodybuilding Supplements
Explained
Jon Shelton
978-1941070239

Demonology
Riley Star
978-19401070314

Pigeon Racing
Lolly Brown
978-1941070307

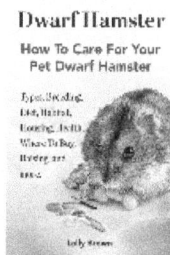

Dwarf Hamster
Lolly Brown
978-1941070390

Cryptozoology
Rex Cutty
978-1941070406

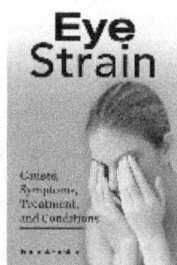

Eye Strain
Frederick Earlstein
978-1941070369

Inez The Miniature Elephant
Asher Ray
978-1941070353

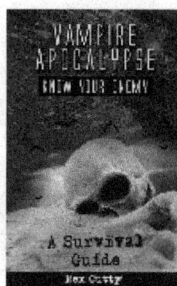

Vampire Apocalypse
Rex Cutty
978-1941070321

www.ingramcontent.com/pod-product-compliance
Lightning Source LLC
LaVergne TN
LVHW051644080426
835511LV00016B/2488